Affirmations

Powerful Affirmations that Work!

Change Your Life for the Better, Positive Thinking at Its Best

Introduction

I want to thank you and congratulate you for purchasing the book, *"Affirmations: Powerful Affirmations that Work! Change Your Life for the Better, Positive Thinking at Its Best"*.

Words are powerful because they shape your reality and they influence your behavior. They influence your subconscious mind and inspire you to take action. They shape your physical reality. So, if you want to make positive changes in your life, you must always say positive words such as affirmations.

Affirmations are positive phrases or sentences that are created to affect the subconscious and conscious mind. They motivate you and keep you focused on your goals. They also change the way you behave and can get you in contact with people that can help you achieve your goals. They make you feel positive, optimistic, hopeful, and enthusiastic. They also inspire you to do whatever you can do in your power to achieve your goals.

This book will help you use the power of words to manifest your dreams and desires. This book contains powerful affirmations that can help you change your life. In this book, you'll find:

- The benefits of affirmations
- A total of 750 affirmations!
- 100 affirmations for love
- 100 affirmations for wealth and abundance
- 150 affirmations for self-confidence and self-esteem
- 150 affirmations for success and empowerment

- 100 affirmations for happiness
- 50 affirmations for travel and adventure
- 50 affirmations for health
- 50 affirmations for healing emotional pain

This book will change your life by changing your thoughts. So, if you're feeling stuck or uninspired, take time to say the powerful affirmations contained in this book and you'll soon see positive changes in your life. These affirmations can bring you anything that you want – happiness, soul mate, success, self-confidence, money, travel, and good health. It is time to change your life by changing your words.

Thanks again for purchasing this book, I hope you enjoy it!

Table of Contents

Chapter 1: The Power of Affirmations

Affirmations are more than just positive words, they are tools you can use to transform your life and manifest your desires. Remember that thoughts become things. So, when you say these affirmations, the universe will conspire to transform these words into reality. Affirmations also transforms you into a magnet, allowing you to attract positive people, things, and events that will help manifest your dreams into your physical reality.

But, aside from manifestation, saying affirmations regularly have a lot of other benefits, including:

- It helps you focus on what you want.

Most people focus on what they don't want. Saying affirmations daily allows you to focus on things that you want. It helps you release your fears, doubts, and negative thoughts. It aligns you with the things that you desire.

- It helps you attract positive events.

  Remember that "like attracts like". So, in order to attract great things and events, it is important to practice positive thinking by reciting affirmations daily.

- It helps alleviate stress.

  Affirmations help alleviate stress that's associated with negative thoughts. Saying affirmations daily helps you look at the brighter side of things. It helps you remove all your worries.

- It makes you glow.

Peter Pan once said "Think happy thoughts and you will fly". Positive thinking makes you glow. It helps you radiate beauty that shines from within. It makes you happier so it also makes you more attractive.

- It is flexible.

You can use affirmations to address various parts of your life. You can use them to attract various things such as love, happiness, health, money, and friends. You can even use these affirmations to achieve academic success, attract your dream vacation, or increase your self-confidence.

- It is empowering.

Affirmations help you recognize your power to change your life. It helps you realize how strong you really are. It also helps you see each experience as a learning opportunity. They help you rise above your mistakes and focus on turning your dream life into a reality.

- It improves your work performance.

  Saying affirmations daily help improve your work performance and focus. It gives you the confidence to take action and take control of your destiny.

- It helps prevent and cure certain mental issues.

  Affirmations empower you. They help you rise above your problems and emotional issues. They give you hope. So, they help you overcome psychological problems such as anxiety and depression. So, if you're feeling down lately, it's a good idea to start reciting empowering affirmations. It also helps you drop your emotional baggage and confidence issues.

- It helps you reach your full potential.

  Affirmations help you reach your full potential. They empower you to use your strengths, talents, and capabilities.

- It helps you silence your inner critic.

  We all have that inner voice telling us we're ugly, fat, stupid, or not good enough. This voice is called your inner critic and it robs you of joy, happiness, and millions of opportunities. Saying positive affirmations to increase your self-belief is a powerful way to silence your inner critic.

How Affirmations Work

There's a part of our brain called Reticular Activating System or RAS, and its job is to filter out all of the information in your brain that you don't need so you're only left with the important bits. It generally filters the information tied to your needs, goals, desires, and interests. So, for example, you're walking on the street with your friend. You're hungry while your friend is looking for a date. Most likely, you'll see all the fast foods and restaurants and your friend will see potential dates or lovers.

So, when you repeat an affirmation over and over again, a number of things happen in your life that could turn that affirmation into a reality. For example, if your affirmation is "I'm going to lose 20 pounds in 3 months", you'll suddenly notice gyms, fit people, and healthy foods. If your affirmation is "I'm going to be a successful businessman", you'll suddenly notice business opportunities.

Tips on Making Your Own Affirmations

This book contains 750 affirmations, but you are not required to use all of them if you don't want to, it is actually better if you can make your own affirmations. Here are some tips on how to come up with your own affirmations:

- Use powerful words.

  Words carry a specific vibration. So, it is important to use powerful words such as "incredible", "amazing", "fantastic", and "wonderful". It is also important to use words that excite you.

- Keep it short.

  It's hard to say a 200 word affirmation. So, it's best to keep it short, concise, and simple. You can say something as simple as "I am happy" or "I am worthy of love".

- Make it personal.

  Always use the words "I", "my", "mine", or "me" when formulating your affirmations.

- Keep your affirmations private.

  It is necessary to keep your affirmations to yourself. However, if you really want to, you can also share them to certain people who support your dreams and desires.

- Say these affirmations consistently.

  To achieve your desired results, you have to say your affirmations consistently and regularly. You must recite these affirmations daily for at least 21 days.

Remember that words are powerful. They have the power to change yourself and your life. If you want to achieve great things, start reciting the 750 affirmations that you can find later in this book. You can also formulate your own affirmations using the tips contained in this chapter.

Chapter 2: 100 Affirmations for Love

All of us want to find love. We all want to share our lives with a special someone. Well, if your goal is to find the love of your life or improve your existing relationship, here are the most powerful affirmations that you can use to manifest love or strengthen your existing relationship:

- I am attracting the love of my life.
- I accept infinite love.
- I love myself.
- I am ready for love.
- I think relationships are fun!
- My relationship is becoming deeper and stronger.
- I accept all the love that's given to me.

- My partner finds me irresistible.
- I have a partner that is madly and deeply in love with me.
- Love is my birthright.
- I deserve to be loved.
- I am love.
- I naturally attract great relationships in my life.
- I open myself to my soul mate.
- I have a funny and loving partner.
- My partner loves me for who I am.
- My soul mate loves me above all else.
- I welcome my soul mate with open arms.
- I am ready to be loved.
- I radiate love.
- I have a peaceful and loving relationship.
- I am ready to meet the perfect partner.
- I radiate pure and unconditional love.

- I feel wonderful about my love life.
- My heart is open for perfect relationships and love.
- I am loveable.
- I am surrounded with loving people.
- I am ready to share my life with the love of my life.
- I am drawn to my soul mate.
- I effortlessly attract love into my life.
- My heart is full with love.
- I attract the love that I want and deserve.
- I am magnetic.
- My partner brings peace to my life.
- I draw life into my life.
- I radiate positive energy.
- I am an amazing person and I deserve love.
- I deserve to be in a happy relationship.

- I have a lot to offer.
- I forgive myself for all the mistakes that I have made.
- I take time to listen to my partner and the people around me.
- I choose relationships that fulfill and uplift me.
- I am blessed that I am surrounded with loving and amazing people.
- I have a strong connection with the person I love
- I am kind, caring, and loving.
- I share my life with the perfect soul mate.
- I am loveable.
- I spiritually connected with my loved one.
- I radiate loving energy.
- I trust my partner.

- I freely give and receive love.
- I have the best soul mate in the world.
- I openly receive love in my life.
- I attract love effortlessly and easily.
- I have the perfect relationship.
- I open my heart to love.
- I am thankful for all the love in my life.
- The more I love myself, the closer I get to my soul mate.
- I am worthy of receiving love.
- I am worthy of receiving love.
- I am compassionate.
- I develop relationships easily.
- I give love fully.
- I attract love effortlessly.
- I am beautiful inside and out.
- I am in a harmonious relationship with my ideal partner.
- My partner is my best friend.

- I share my life with a loving partner.
- My soul mate and I are compatible sexually, emotionally, intellectually, spiritually, and physically.
- I radiate pure love.
- I give unconditional love to my partner.
- My life is balanced.
- I respect my partner.
- My partner respects me.
- I believe in my partner.
- My partner believes in me.
- I listen to my soul mate with genuine interest.
- I am in the right place and at the right time.
- I have a caring partner.
- My partner brings peace to my mind.
- I am worthy of pure love.
- I effortlessly radiate loving energy.

- My partner prioritizes me.
- I have a supportive partner.
- I open my doors to love and new relationships.
- I attract healthy relationships.
- I release my past pain and I am ready to open my life to love.
- I open myself to true love.
- I have a happy love life.
- I will find the right partner soon.
- I have a patient and loving partner.
- I am destined to be in the perfect relationship.
- I have a fun and playful partner.
- I love to experience new things with my soul mate.
- I have a partner who has a strong character and integrity.

- I am focused on attracting the perfect partner.
- I am open to fun, happiness, and love.
- I love being with my soul mate – my other half.
- I attract unconditional love in everything that I do.
- My life is filled with romance.

As mentioned before, you need not recite all 100 of these affirmations, just choose the ones that feel right for you. Once you've chosen your affirmations, recite them in the morning when you wake up and at night before going to sleep. For best results, hold a rose quartz near your heart while reciting these love affirmations.

Chapter 3: 100 Powerful Affirmations for Wealth and Abundance

All of us want to earn more money. If you have been having financial problems lately, you can use the following 100 powerful affirmations that will help manifest wealth and prosperity in your life:

- I love money and money loves me back.
- I am a money magnet.
- I am in the process of attracting more money into my life.
- I feel rich.
- I see abundance everywhere I go.
- I manage my finances wisely.
- My income is getting higher and higher.
- My bank balance is increasing each day.

- The money in my bank account is growing.
- I attract more money into my life.
- I focus my energy on becoming rich.
- I think that money is good.
- I appreciate all the money that I have.
- I enjoy life using the money that I make.
- I naturally attract money.
- Money is in love with me.
- I have a stable financial life.
- I am lucky.
- I am experiencing financial success.
- My business is growing.
- I live a prosperous life.
- I am grateful for my wealth.
- I pay all my bills all time.
- I attract money everywhere I go.
- I enjoy making money.
- Money flows freely into my life.

- I feel good about spending money.
- I am wealthy.
- I am a good money manager.
- I always have more than I need.
- I attract money easily.
- My pockets are always full.
- I welcome more money into my life.
- I have good fortune.
- I am a money magnet.
- I am fearless.
- I live in a prosperous world.
- Money makes me feel good.
- I welcome all the things that I can buy.
- Money has a positive energy.
- I am worthy of wealth.
- I accept all the wealth that the universe is sending my way.
- I have the ability to generate wealth.
- I love money-= activities.

- I am a gifted entrepreneur.
- I choose abundance.
- I am happy and wealthy.
- All the forces in the universe are conspiring in making me wealthy.
- I create wealth.
- I focus my energy on money-=making tasks.
- I use my wealth to help others.
- I focus on success.
- I have a charmed life.
- I am always willing to give more than what I'm paid for.
- I am prosperous and positive.
- I live an abundant life.
- I attract abundance.
- I am a goldmine.
- I accept abundance.
- I am destined to be prosperous.

- I choose to live an abundant life.
- I always have all I need.
- I am attracted to money.
- My life is overflowing with money.
- I now live in a rich universe.
- I always have enough money.
- I never run out of money.
- I let go of all my negative perceptions about money.
- I have the power to attract prosperity and wealth.
- I embrace wealth.
- Being rich gives me joy.
- I love being rich.
- I live a luxurious life.
- I deserve prosperity.
- I thank the universe for all the wealth in my life.
- My net worth is getting bigger each day.

- I create prosperity easily.
- I am living a prosperous life.
- I accept all the wealth that the universe has to offer.
- I live an easy life.
- I deserve more money.
- I have wonderful money-making ideas.
- I always have enough money.
- I am worthy of success.
- I live a luxurious life.
- I can afford expensive things.
- I have everything I need.
- I radiate prosperity.
- Attracting money is easy for me.
- I always think positive thoughts about wealth and money.
- I am becoming richer and richer each day.
- I see prosperity wherever I turn.

- I am an unlimited being.
- My wallet is filled with hundred dollar bills.
- I find happiness in prosperity.
- My life is filled with good fortune.
- I think happy thoughts about money.
- I am debt-free.
- I am open to new moneymaking opportunities.
- I have a strong friendship with money.

You can say these affirmations before you start your work in the morning and before you sleep at night. To get fast results, it is important to say these affirmations with faith and conviction.

Chapter 4: 150 Affirmations for Success and Empowerment

Success does not only bring you popularity and prestige. It also gives you a strong sense of fulfillment. It gives you the power to influence people. If you want to be successful in your business and career, here's a list of powerful affirmations that will condition your mind and prepare you for success:

- I am successful.
- I am grateful for all the positive things that are happening in my life.
- I am fearless.
- I am lucky in my career.
- I find it easy to achieve my goal.
- I am passionate about my work.
- I have an amazing life.

- I work for my dreams.
- I am energetic and enthusiastic.
- I deserve success.
- I am successful in all areas of my life.
- I am incredibly successful.
- I am resilient.
- I look at failures are opportunities.
- I am wealthy and happy.
- I know what I want and how to achieve it.
- I am powerful and strong.
- I am in charge of my life.
- I am planting the seeds of my success.
- I always do my best.
- I am a big success.
- I am the best at what I do.
- I am well-paid.
- My business is growing.
- I slowly rise to the top.

- I am passionate and I deserve success.
- The level of my success is increasing every day.
- I am enthusiastic.
- I am in charge of my life.
- Everybody is drawn to me because I radiate positive energy.
- It's easy for me to move forward and achieve my goals.
- I am persistent and determine.
- I am disciplined.
- I deserve to be successful.
- I forgive myself for my past failures and I am now ready for success.
- I create my opportunities.
- I am fulfilling my life's purpose.
- I am energized and inspired by the challenges in my business.
- I am a talented entrepreneur.

- I am enjoying massive success.
- I treasure my success.
- I am talented.
- I am intelligent.
- I am admired.
- I can make my dream come true.
- I am surrounded with opportunities.
- I am not too old to chase my goals and dreams.
- I refuse to give up on my dreams.
- I enjoy my work.
- I am an expert.
- I use my skills and talents to achieve success.
- I believe in my ability to succeed.
- I surround myself with people who believe in me.
- I am powerful, calm, and confident.
- I am a problem-solver.

- I trust my intuition.
- I take pride in what I do.
- I dress for success.
- I thrive under pressure.
- I love my job.
- I see prosperity everywhere I look.
- I am creating solutions for my problems.
- I am not afraid of success.
- I am open to success.
- I open my heart to success.
- I committed to my career.
- I am releasing all my fears.
- I am getting closer and closer to my dreams.
- I attract success in everything that I do.
- I spend my days doing the things that I love.
- There are no limits to what I could achieve.

- My life is filled with success and good fortune.
- Success is my birthright.
- I deserve success.
- I am a success magnet.
- Success is a part of my life.
- I am reaching my goals every day.
- I deserve to reach my goals.
- Everything is working out for me.
- I accomplish everything that I set out to do.
- I reach my goals easily.
- I am getting closer and closer to my dreams each day.
- I aspire for greater things.
- I am determined.
- I can do it.
- I am persistent.
- I am empowered.

- I am making the decision to follow my dreams.
- I take firm actions towards my goals.
- I have incredible self-control.
- I am the master of my habits.
- I am willing to change habits to achieve success.
- I am destined to be great.
- I am powerful.
- I see success in everything I do.
- I take time to celebrate my success.
- I chase opportunities.
- I am inspired.
- I work hard to be the best that I can be.
- I easily attract success and opportunities.
- I do more than what's expected.
- I deserve to be on the top.
- I am confident and certain.

- I succeed with ease.
- I move forward eagerly.
- Abundance surrounds me.
- I live on purpose.
- I will not care what other people think.
- I will try to be better.
- My dream is coming true right now.
- I am not too old to set a new dream or goal.
- I have the power to make my dreams come true.
- The possibilities are endless.
- I find it easy to fulfill my dreams.
- Nothing will stop me from achieving my dreams.
- I am surrounded with people who can help me achieve success.
- I am a magnet and I attract success.
- I act fearlessly.

- I have an amazing life.
- I find it easy to succeed in everything I do.
- I am decisive.
- I take action.
- I continuously enjoy every area of my life.
- The universe always provides for me.
- I am ambitious and motivated.
- My dreams are coming true.
- I am dedicated.
- I am incredibly committed to my goals and dreams.
- There's nothing that I cannot do.
- I can move mountains using the power of my love.
- I am in charge of every aspect of my life.
- I am smart enough to figure out a way to fulfill my dreams.

- I dress for success.
- I believe in my ability to succeed.
- I trust my intuition.
- I always expect a positive outcome.
- I stop outside my comfort zone.
- I have the power to change my life.
- I easily find solutions to my problems.
- I am following my life purpose.
- I have the power to achieve my goals.
- Every task that I complete brings me closer to my goals.
- I am moving closer to my goals everyday.
- I focus on my goals.
- I do whatever it takes to achieve my goals.
- I am 100% committed to my goals.
- I set inspiring, but realistic goals.
- I have faith in myself and talents.

- I will achieve business success.
- I am living my dream.

Remember to say these affirmations with conviction and faith. Recite these affirmations once or twice a day for the next 21 days.

Chapter 5: 150 Affirmations for Self-confidence and Self-Esteem

High self-esteem allows you to live a happy and meaningful life. It allows you to attract positive relationships and opportunities. Having high self-esteem and self-confidence also increases your changes of being successful in life. It increases your resilience and it enhances your ability to manage stress. It also makes you more attractive.

To increase your self-confidence and self-esteem, say these affirmations at least once a day for the next 21 days:

- I am loveable.
- I am desirable.
- I make my own decisions and choices.
- I am in control of my life.

- I am the master of my life.
- I am worthy of love and success.
- I am confident.
- I believe in myself.
- I am in love with myself.
- I am bold.
- I am outgoing.
- I am self-reliant.
- I am creative.
- I have the ability to create the life that I want.
- I can easily adjust to different situations.
- I am healthy and full of confidence.
- I am a good problem solver.
- I fill my mind with positive thoughts.
- I love exercising my body.
- I am at peace with myself.
- I take care of myself.
- I deserve nothing but the best.

- I am strong and gentle.
- I am a quick learner.
- I take care of my body.
- I have strong belief in myself.
- I have faith in my abilities.
- I am worthy of all the happiness in life.
- I am loveable and likeable.
- I am trustworthy.
- I am strong.
- I make sound decisions.
- I deserve all the beautiful things in life.
- I deserve success and happiness.
- I deserve to be treated well.
- I am a valuable person.
- I am caring.
- Public speaking is easy for me.
- I am attractive.
- I am beautiful.
- I radiate confidence.

- I love challenges because it brings out the best of me.
- My life is rewarding and fun.
- I can make my own choices.
- I have the power to change my life.
- I deserve to successful.
- I am a remarkable human being.
- I am a wonderful person.
- I am a talented person.
- I am unique.
- I am comfortable in my own skin.
- My opinion matters.
- I am excellent.
- I am kind to myself.
- I am free to say no to requests that make me uncomfortable.
- I feel amazing.
- I inhale confidence and exhale shyness.
- I love meeting strangers.

- I am comfortable when I'm around people.
- I am self-reliant.
- I am a great problem-solver.
- I move with purpose.
- I am self-assured.
- I am in control.
- I am proud of who I am and what I have become over the years.
- I am confident when I'm around people.
- I am wise.
- I am a principled person.
- I move with poise and confidence.
- I stand tall.
- My life is rewarding.
- The task at hand is difficult, but I can do this.
- I truly care for others.
- I am reliable and I have integrity.

- I am determined and persistent.
- I am special.
- I have the ability to grow.
- I can change my situation.
- I am in the driver seat of my life.
- I control my fate.
- I am not damaged.
- I am worthy of joy, love, happiness, and wealth.
- I am adventurous and wise.
- I act with confidence and courage.
- I am brave to face the unknown.
- No one could shake my confidence.
- I feed my mind with positive thoughts daily.
- I deserve to get what I want.
- I am powerful and centered.
- My life is an exciting adventure.

- The people in my life are lucky to have me.
- My limitations are only in my mind.
- I let go of all the negative thoughts.
- I am capable of making the best decisions.
- I am capable of reaching my dreams.
- I am competent and I can get the job done.
- I feel great about who I am.
- I am a well-respected person.
- I focus on solutions.
- I am in charge of my actions, thoughts, and words.
- I am an excellent worker.
- I deserve to be treated well by the people around me.
- I am grateful for my uniqueness.
- I am terrific.

- I am proud of what I'm doing for a living.
- I am the best in my industry.
- I am appreciated by the people around me.
- I am a creator of my own destiny.
- I inhale confidence.
- I release all my insecurities.
- I am healthy and well-groomed.
- Confidence is my second nature.
- I fill my mind with positive thoughts.
- My inner wisdom is increasing every day.
- I am secure with myself.
- I am at peace with who I am.
- I am at ease with myself.
- I am enough.
- I am worth more than my weight or appearance.

- I can succeed in everything I put my mind into.
- I am growing more and more beautiful each day.
- I am a gift to the universe.
- I love and approve of myself.
- I am a unique child of the world.
- Wonderful things are happening to me.
- I trust myself and I know that I have the wisdom and intelligence to make the right decision.
- I am happy with who I am.
- I can say no.
- I am in the process of creating the perfect version of myself.
- I am blessed beyond measure.
- I am secure and strong.
- Many people admire me because of my talents and confidence.

- I am calm even when faced with a difficult situation.
- I use my personal power to shape my reality.
- I am competent and intelligent.
- I can clearly communicate my needs.
- I refuse to change myself just to gain the approval of others.
- I am adventurous and wise.
- I use my time wisely.
- I am centered and powerful.
- I invest my time in activities that help me grow and develop as a person.
- I have strong self-control.
- I am doing things effortlessly.
- I can learn and master just about anything.
- I am an honest person.
- I love my body fully and deeply.

- I am a good person.
- I am not perfect, but I am doing my best.
- I am growing more beautiful each day.
- I believe that I deserve to have it all.

Having a high self-esteem can help you build honest and strong relationships. It increases your confidence and it helps you bounce back from your setbacks easily.

Chapter 6: 100 Affirmations for Happiness

We all want to be happy. But, if finding happiness is a challenge for you, you can use these 100 powerful affirmations for happiness:

- I am happy.
- I have everything that I need.
- I choose to think nothing but happy thoughts.
- My life is an adventure.
- I enjoy every minute of the day.
- I am grateful for everything in my life.
- I love making people happy.
- I have a wonderful life.
- I have a happy disposition.
- I touch many lives.

- I have the ability to brighten other people's day.
- I am the architect of my life.
- I am compassionate.
- I have limitless possibilities.
- My life is filled with joy.
- I radiate grace and beauty
- I always choose to see the bright side of things.
- I am cheerful.
- I am a positive person.
- I am becoming happier and happier each day.
- I smile often.
- I love making new friends.
- I always follow my bliss.
- My days are filled with happiness and laughter.

- I am happy with the choices that I made in life.
- I am joy in motion.
- I find happiness in whatever I do.
- I carry joyful thoughts whenever I go.
- I find something funny in every situation.
- I enjoy the little joys in life.
- I have a sense of wonder.
- I find joy in little things.
- I embrace the new day with joy and happiness.
- Happiness comes from within.
- I create my own happiness.
- I do not take myself seriously.
- I love exchanging jokes with my loved one.
- I follow my bliss.
- I laugh my heart out.

- I smile to everyone I meet.
- I am a naturally cheerful person.
- I lift people up using positive words.
- My life is filled with bliss.
- I always think happy thoughts.
- I am a blessing to everyone around me.
- Happiness is second nature to me.
- I am in charge of my own happiness.
- I bring joy to everyone around me.
- I am joyful.
- I am joy.
- My life is filled with laughter.
- I have enough.
- I am happy with who I am and what I have become.
- I am blessed without measure.
- I enjoy each day as if it's my last.
- I love making other people happy.
- I am happy with my relationships.

- I love my job.
- Happiness is a journey and not a destination.
- Happiness comes easy.
- Kindness breeds love and love breeds happiness.
- I am kind to every person I meet.
- I choose to see the good in people.
- I am connected with my inner child.
- My laugh is contagious.
- I dedicate my life in making others happy.
- I believe that happiness is an inside job.
- For me, happiness is a journey and not a destination.
- I am destined to be happy.
- I am positive.
- I am optimistic.
- I enjoy the little things in life.

- I love being myself.
- Things are getting better each day.
- I let go of things that I cannot change.
- I let go of all my fears and worries.
- I think happy thoughts everyday.
- I am grateful for all the blessings that I now enjoy.
- I work hard, but I also play hard. Life is all about balance.
- I am brimming with positive energy and joy.
- I take time to relax.
- I fill my days with fun activities.
- I focus on things that makes me happy.
- I let go of all my negative thoughts and doubt.
- I am a big ball of joy and happiness.
- I can tap into my inner happiness anytime I want.

- I have a good sense of humor.
- I love my life.
- I am getting happier and happier each day.
- I love meeting strangers.
- I always attract the best of circumstances.
- My life is great.
- I use humor to lift myself up in times of difficulties.
- I experience a strong surge of joy each time I wake up in the morning.
- All is well in my life.
- I am happy at this very moment.
- I take time to appreciate the little things in life.
- I attract positive people.
- I live a life that's full of happiness and bliss.

- Life is good.

We all deserve happiness, so if you're down and out, get up and say these affirmations daily for the next 21 days.

Chapter 7: 100 Affirmations for Travel and Adventure

Traveling is good for you. It allows you to tap your adventurous spirit. It also allows you to experience and learn new things. It also enhances your life skills and it allows you to meet interesting people.

If your dream is to travel around the world, here are the affirmations that you can use:

- I will travel around the world.
- I am surrounded with opportunities that involve travel.
- I enjoy absolute freedom in everything I do.
- I am surrounded by expensive and luxurious items.

- I can afford all the luxuries in the world.
- I experience miracles each day.
- I am a wise traveler.
- I can travel wherever I want and whenever I want.
- I love traveling.
- I travel safely.
- I am protected by my Guardian Angel whenever I travel.
- I feel joy whenever I travel.
- I arrive at my destination safely and without delays.
- I enjoy traveling around the world.
- My life is filled with adventure.
- I can afford my dream vacation.
- I enjoy planning my vacation.
- I deserve a vacation.
- I travel smoothly.

- The universe is always keeping me safe whenever I'm travelling.

- I am a citizen of the world and I am destined to travel.

- The world is my home and I am ready to explore it.

- I have an adventurous spirit.

- I arrive at my destination safely and in one piece.

- Every place I visit is my home.

- I travel for business and for pleasure.

- I am ready to try new things.

- I am ready to visit a new place.

- I am happiest when I'm traveling.

- I love to explore the different beaches in the world.

- I find joy in visiting different cultural spots.

- I am not afraid to try new things.

- I am fun.
- I look forward to experiencing something new.
- I love eating exotic foods whenever I travel.
- I am ready to step out of my comfort zone.
- I love meeting local people.
- I love taking photos while I'm travelling.
- Traveling helps me learn new things.
- I can afford to visit the most beautiful places in the world.
- I am blessed with travel opportunities.
- It's time for another adventure.
- Traveling is the best way to learn.
- The world is mine.
- I love going to places I've never been before.

- Visiting a new place gives me a strong feeling of joy.
- I am spontaneous.
- I enjoy adventure trips.
- I live an exciting life.
- My life is an adventure.

Cut out photos of the places you want to go to. Look at the photos while saying these affirmations. This technique expedites the effect of the affirmations.

Chapter 8: 50 Affirmations for Health and Fitness

We all deserve to be healthy. The following affirmations can help increase your health and fitness:

- I am healthy.
- I am filled with energy.
- I am in perfect health.
- My body is perfect as it is.
- I enjoy my body.
- Every cell in my body is healthy.
- I feed my body with healthy food.
- I exercise daily.
- I eat nothing but fruits and vegetables.
- It is easy for me to let go of my unhealthy habits.
- Healthy eating is my way of life.

- I feel healthier everytime I breathe.
- I am fit, strong, and healthy.
- I express gratitude for my health.
- I am strong.
- I deserve a fit body.
- I deserve to be healthy.
- I am getting healthier each day.
- I am getting fitter each day.
- I love running.
- I love doing yoga and other exercises.
- I do my best to keep myself healthy.
- I have an amazing body.
- I feel healthy and fabulous.
- Exercising makes me feel fantastic.
- I can move easily.
- My body is becoming leaner and stronger.
- I am becoming younger and fitter.
- I am healthy and attractive.

- I replace dieting with healthy eating.
- I choose to change my eating habits.
- I am transforming my body.
- I am becoming a better version of myself.
- I am beautiful and healthy.
- I am attractive and fit.
- My health is at its peak.
- I am grateful for my good health.
- I am healthy and well in body, mind, and spirit.
- I feel good whenever I exercise.
- I choose to focus on my health.
- I find it easy to pick healthy choices.
- My stamina increases each day.
- I am blessed with a healthy body.
- I am well and healthy.
- I inhale confidence and exhale fear.
- The scale does not define me.

- I choose to be healthy.
- I get all the vitamins and nutrients that I need.
- I love being healthy.
- I am glowing with health and vitality.

Chapter 9: 50 Emotional Healing Affirmations

Getting over a traumatic event can be challenging, but you can get over them if you have the right attitude. These affirmations can help heal deep-seated emotional wounds and help you get over a breakup, emotional or physical abuse, or a traumatic event:

- I see problems as opportunities.
- I am getting stronger and wiser.
- I forgive myself for all the bad decisions that I have made in the past.
- I am compassionate and loving.
- I have the ability to rise above heartbreaks.
- When a door closes, another door opens.

- I am strong and vulnerable at the same time.
- This will pass.
- The Divine Energy will heal my wounds.
- I release all my anger.
- I rise above all the emotional abuse that I have experienced.
- I am valuable and I choose to believe in myself.
- I am optimistic about the future.
- I will push myself up.
- I let go of rejection.
- I choose to see an emotional rejection as an opportunity to find something better.
- I choose to let go of my emotional pain.
- I choose to re-invent myself.
- I choose to forget the past and move forward.
- I am important and I am beautiful.

- I let go of all my worries, regrets, and insecurities.
- I choose to take the high road.
- I treat myself with self-respect.
- I spend my days on things that energizes me and avoid things that drains me.
- Sometimes bad things happen to good people. It's okay.
- A crisis sharpens me and reveals my true brilliance.
- I am awesome. I can get over this.
- It is not too late to start over.
- I choose to heal my broken heart.
- I choose to let go of the pain associated with my past.
- I am grateful for all my pain because they made me stronger.
- I am not a sob story.
- I am not a victim. I am a winner.

- I can use my emotional pain as a drive to succeed.
- I am worthy of all the good things in life.
- I choose hope.
- I let go of my anger because it is not good for me.
- Forgiveness comes naturally for me.
- I choose to forgive because it's good for me.
- I move away from my past.
- I choose to let go the negative memories.
- I forgive all the people around me including myself.
- I forgive myself for all the terrible things that I have done in the past.
- I release all my anger, pain, and resentment.
- I am ready to move forward.
- I am excited to see what lies ahead.

- I heal my pain.
- I let go of all my emotional issues. I now open myself up for success and happiness.
- Past is past. My abusers can no longer hurt me.
- I choose to accept the apology I never got.

You do not have to live in the past. To create a happy, successful, and fulfilling life, you need to let go of your emotional baggage and open yourself up to emotional healing.

Conclusion

Thank you again for purchasing this book!

I hope that the affirmations contained in this book has helped you improve the several aspects of your life.

The next step is to continue to continue to use these affirmations to achieve your goals and your dreams. But, while affirmations can help increase the synchronicities in your life, it will not work unless you take action. So, while it is important to say these affirmations. It is also equally important to stay alert to the opportunities and take action.

Finally, if you enjoyed this book, then I'd like to ask you for a favor, would you be kind enough to leave a review for this book on Amazon? It'd be greatly appreciated!

Thank you and good luck!